MY LIFE WITHOUT

CRYSTAL HOLROYD

ISBN 978-1-68517-143-8 (paperback)
ISBN 978-1-68517-144-5 (digital)

Christian Faith Publishing, Inc.
832 Park Avenue
Meadville, PA 16335
www.christianfaithpublishing.com

Printed in the United States of America

CHAPTER 1

The Monster

Well, I didn't ask to be born. Nobody ever asks to be born. I knew I wasn't planned because my mom and my dad were very young. My dad was a warrant officer overseas at the time, and my mom was nineteen and pregnant with me. While my dad was overseas, he ended up meeting another woman while he was still married to my mom. He continued his relationship overseas and married the Korean woman. My mom was left abandoned at nineteen years old. At that time, she liked to drink. She passed away on February 15, 2018, and I never got to ask her, but I'm pretty sure she told me she didn't drink while she was pregnant with me. I do know that I was not planned. I believe I am here for a great purpose!

After about a year, my father tried coming to see me while my mom was living at her parents' house in Lunenburg, Massachusetts, where they were both from. My grandfather was standing at the door holding a shotgun and telling him to go away. My father was never to be seen again. Now here I am, abandoned and fatherless. My mother began to lose her mind, and she didn't want to be my mother anymore. She decided to drink and do drugs because she felt abandoned herself. She became very neglectful with me. She would leave me in the sink long enough to where the water got cold. She would also leave me all alone while she went out with her friends. She was always high or drunk, while I was screaming and crying.

One day my grandparents came home and saw what was happening. They called DCF and had me pulled out of my home. I just found out this past year that I was put in a foster home until I was at the age of two. My grandparents wouldn't take me, but my mother's sister did. She was twenty years old at the time and married to a man who was a few years older than her. She said that she didn't want to see me outside the family, so that's why she wanted to take me. Well, here I am, getting older, and I'm thinking I have a great life. I had everything I wanted.

I remember living in a two-family house in Fitchburg Mass. My aunt loved to play cards with her friends. This is what I could remember. I was jumping on the bed just like a four- or five-year-old would. It was the first time my uncle came into the room, and he began to kiss me. I was not talking about a kiss on the forehead or a kiss on the cheek. He pretty much taught me how to French kiss. I didn't understand, and I thought this was normal. I was a kid, and that's when I began thinking this is what is supposed to happen.

From there, it progressed. Every time my aunt would go out, I knew he would come around and do something else. I didn't remember anything that bad, but I did know it was bad enough where I knew an adult man shouldn't be kissing a five-year-old girl in that kind of way.

We moved from that apartment and ended up in a house with a swimming pool where there was always lots of family activity. I began to think my life was safe now because I found out my biological mother lived only ten minutes away. She was trying to come back into my life, but she was still active with her drinking. Now she was a full-blown alcoholic. I was around eight years old when she came knocking at the door, hollering and shouting, "Where is my daughter?"

I had to watch her and my aunt fight, because my aunt didn't want me to see her in that state. My mother pushed my aunt and forced her way into the house as my aunt shouted at me to get in my room. My mother was flipping our dining room chairs while screaming my name. I was in my room crying and scared.

When I heard silence, my aunt said, "You can come out now, the idiot is gone."

My mom always wore leather jackets, high-heeled boots, and lots of makeup. I hated the smell of leather and booze!

Now back to my uncle. For a brief time, I thought I was safe having my mom try to come back into my life. Unfortunately, this was not the case. He would come in spurts. He would touch me and then not touch me. In this house, it ended up getting worse. He would set the alarm clock and get up extra early so he would not wake up my aunt. He would hit the alarm button right away, but I always heard it. I was in third grade at the time, so I should have been up around seven o'clock, but instead I was woken up an hour early.

He would come in and sit on the edge of my bed and call my name quietly and kind of tug at me to wake me. I would try my hardest to pretend that I was sound asleep, but he would lift me up by my back and sit me up on him in a straddle position. This was new to me, so I had to go along with it because I was scared. When I was on top of what you would call a man's penis, he forced me back and forth on him in what I know now as an adult is called humping.

I remember him always telling me how beautiful I was and how I felt good. He never actually had sex with me, but either way, this really messed my life up. I blocked it out because I started to realize that adults do these things.

This continued for months, and when I heard a noise, I was excited thinking it was either my aunt waking up to save me or him getting caught. It was what I had hoped for: for this nightmare to end. She never came. I was a little eight-year-old girl all alone with this monster. When it was happening, I would turn numb. I didn't feel real. It was almost as if I left my own body, if you could understand that. I would have to get up every day, go to school like every other kid, and play pretend. Here I am a third grader hoping that my mother will come and save me, but she was still a negligent alcoholic.

I also did not have my aunt because he was telling me to keep this our little secret. That is when I finally began to realize this was very bad. It got to the point where everything I ever wanted, I received. He was a very wealthy business owner and knew a lot of people. He owned a very popular garage and did a lot of car racing. A lot of people thought very highly of him.

His abuse continued, but it started to change. He would now come in the room to scold me for doing something wrong. When he did, he would force my pants down and spank me in a sexual way while smacking me across his knee. I knew I was too old at this point to be spanked in this kind of way. I remember having a huge piggy bank, and it became my focal point while I would get spanked. It became a ritual, and I would just feel like I was dreaming. I started to hide as much as I could. I would be at my grandparents' almost every weekend, or I would always be at a friend's house. I didn't want him to come around me or to even come near me. I was always in fear of what he would do, and I continued to not understand.

As I got older, the abuse had stopped between the ages of eleven and thirteen. I can't remember exactly at what age it stopped because it was like I just blocked everything out. He abused me continuously from the ages of four through thirteen. I didn't want to remember it, but I do remember it was a repeated nightmare. To all of you out there that has had this happen to them or know someone out there who is being abused, I pray for all of you because you are not alone.

CHAPTER 2
The Truth Comes Out

I'm now in eighth grade, and the abuse has lessened. He's more distant because he knows I'm older and can report it at any time. I was thirteen and a half going on fourteen when I started to date. My first boyfriend would pick me up, and we would hang out. (I was fourteen and allowed to be picked up by a sixteen-year-old boy.) He was captain of the football team, and my uncle was jealous.

My uncle would say nasty things to me like calling me a whore and "You're too young to be getting into cars with boys." After he started speaking to me like that, I always made sure my best friend was with me, because I didn't want him to speak to me that way. She knew what was going on and what he did to me.

One night she and I were in my room changing into our pajamas when he opened the door. We both screamed, "Get out!" and he said in a soft voice, "Oops, sorry."

He was hoping to get a glimpse of my maturing body. When my friends started to find out what was happening in my life, they became protective of me. They were always around me, and the male friends that I had were always making sure I was never alone with the monster.

One night he called me into the living room. He told me to come sit on his lap. Remember, I was now fourteen years old. I asked him why I should sit on his lap. He proceeded to tell me it's because my breasts were getting bigger and that I was starting to look like a woman. He told me I was going to be somebody's someday and started to sexually molest me with his words.

At that point, I got so upset that I left with a friend and didn't come back that night. The following day, my friend and I called another aunt of mine. I told her she needed to pick me up and that we needed to talk.

We went to a public restaurant with another close family friend. I then told them what had been happening to me since I was little. I finally came forward with tears in my eyes full of shame and embarrassment. Their jaws dropped to the ground. It was as if someone had died. We then called my aunt, who was married to this monster. I didn't want her to know because I was scared. They said, "No, this is serious, and she needs to know."

When she arrived, I told her everything, and she said, "You're lying, this has got to be a joke."

She said that I was just looking for attention and that if it weren't for the clothes that I'm wearing, he wouldn't be trying to molest me. I told her, "No, he's been doing this since I was a little girl."

She told me she didn't care and that I was making this all up and she believed it was one big fat lie. I now had to cry and mourn with two people other than the person whom I thought loved me.

It was very devastating because I was now all by myself emotionally. I was beside myself. I've now come clean and have gone to someone I thought I could trust and believe me, my own blood. Her response was that he was so good to me and he had given me everything that I needed. She just didn't care.

As hard as I cried in this public place, she only believed it was just for attention. I believed it was just shock and this was her reaction. She was lied to and deceived by a man whom she thought she was going to be with for the rest of her life. In her eyes, I had ruined that.

I had to go back to that house and continued to live around two people whom I thought loved me: one who loved me the wrong way and the other who neglected to see my pain. How uncomfortable was that! I began to question whether or not to pack my bags, wondering if I should call someone or stay with my best friend. I just kept asking myself, *What do I do?*

All I was trying to do was to live my life as a normal teenager, go to school, and concentrate on graduating while trying to have fun with my friends.

Now that everything was out, he came to me and threatened me. He told me that if I told anyone outside of our small circle, he would kill me. Now I was scared out of my mind. He was a well-known, respected man. How was I supposed to go up against this kind of man? I couldn't believe he continued to live in this house.

At this point, they had been married for fifteen years. They were now getting a divorce not because he had abused me but because he had admitted that he had been cheating on my aunt with another woman. This woman had a daughter who was at a younger age, and I was scared for her. He was looking for a new victim. I became a detective and had to find out who this woman was and get to her daughter as soon as I could.

I don't remember how long it took me to meet her, but when I did, I took her daughter in another room and asked her if he ever did anything to her where she knew it was wrong. She replied, "He tried," and she told him to never touch her like that again or she would tell her mom. I became close to her and her mother, and we remain close to this day.

CHAPTER 3

The Lost Girl

After the monster left, I was now living alone with my aunt, who was still mourning the loss of the defiler. I was now fifteen going on sixteen years old but actually felt as if I was in my twenties. My aunt was starting to date, and so was I. I was going out with my friends all the time while she was trying to find herself again. I now had a lot of freedom because she was never home. I was always drinking, partying, and smoking weed. We had a barrel full of nips in my house. A friend of mine came over after school, and we mixed three different kinds of whiskey with fruit punch. We didn't know what we were doing, but we did it anyway. My friend got so drunk that her eyes rolled back in her head and she fell and whacked her head on my bathtub. I didn't know what to do, so I ran out the door. I didn't call the police, but I knocked on my neighbor's door.

The next thing I know, there were about five people surrounding me. Someone called 911, and she ended up in the hospital with alcohol poisoning. Now seeing this, I had thought I would never have another drink. Of course it didn't work that way. It became more of a habit and something I became tolerant to.

The boy I was dating at the time had me over quite often. He always had people at the house, and the booze was always readily available. This is where I lost my virginity at a very early age. I got to hang around with all the people who were popular, and in turn, I became quite the snob. I was very materialistic and covered up the dark, ugly monster that continued to plague my mind. I had everything I ever could have wanted including cars and name-brand clothing. The monster must've thought he could buy me. To look at me as a stranger, someone from the outside, I looked very put together. No one could have possibly known the deep scars that had been cut.

Now two years later, I started to hang out with another crowd since we had moved after the divorce. I started going to a new high school where there were seven different towns that went to this one vocational high school. Now I was no longer dating the captain of the football team. I was a freshman and started in the middle of the year. I took classes for nursing and enjoyed what I did. I liked being single because now I could focus on myself and my future.

One day a friend of mine approached me and told me that this particular boy, who was a junior, wanted to meet me in the hallway. I wrote a note for her to give to him, and we met later that day. When I saw him, I thought I was living in a dream. This guy was the most gorgeous specimen of a human being that I had ever seen. When we met eye to eye, it was a high-school-sweetheart-love-at-first-sight experience.

In the meantime, my aunt had met someone new and was never home. My boyfriend and I had the house to ourselves, almost as if he and I had our own place. I grew up very fast during that relationship. My aunt would give me money to go grocery shopping, and my boyfriend would take me. We were teenagers playing house, even though he was not allowed to spend the night.

One night he had climbed up my porch to the second floor and tapped on my bedroom window. The next morning, my aunt knocked on my door, which was locked. She needed to use my hair dryer. I told him to get off my bed and hide on the side of it on the floor. I got out of bed and gave her the hair dryer. She then left for work, and my boyfriend and I got to spend the rest of the day together.

This was a perfect example of how she really had no idea of what was going on in my life. I was telling you about all of these relationships because they were very important to understand how I could not stay stable. I could not erase all the old memories and baggage of my childhood that haunted me.

We started going to keg parties and house parties, and as you would know, that's where all the craziness happen. I started to smoke cigarettes, and he didn't smoke. He tried many times to crush my cigarettes and flick them out of my hand. He started to become very controlling. He always wanted to know where I was and made sure it was known that I was his girlfriend. I gave him my house key so he had access to my house at any time.

One day I had forgotten he had a key. He called me and asked me what I was doing. I told him I wasn't feeling well and that I was lying in bed. I lied to him because I just needed some space. My friends were actually on their way to pick me up to go on a pot ride. I stuffed my bed with pillows and made it look like I was in bed sleeping. I even put a pan beside my bed. When I came home from being out with my friends, they waited to make sure I got into the house.

As I got to the door and was ready to put the key in the lock, I heard, "Hey."

I looked up, and there he was in my mother's bedroom hanging out the window with the pan full of cold water. He dumped it on me while my friends watched in the car. I knew right there and then this relationship was getting out of hand at such a young age.

The following day at school, a close friend of mine approached me and told me that he was cheating on me. I called her a liar and told her she was just jealous of our relationship. I started slandering her by telling everyone what she had told me. It got back to her, so she called me and asked me what my problem was. Now this had turned into a physical altercation where she wanted to fight me.

I met her at her house where she was waiting for me at the door. She was wearing her boyfriend's class ring, which was huge, and sucker punched me in the eye. I had my best friend with me, and we both went into her house and ganged up on her. The fight wasn't horrible, but it was to the point where it left us both bleeding. I then confronted my boyfriend, and it was true the whole time. Now that's two relationships where I was cheated on. How are we, as girls, supposed to be secure when it just seems like nothing is ever true?

I was now moving back to Leominster. I was a junior and going to another vocational school. I tried to stay at the school I was already at but it was not allowed. I never had a problem finding new friends at each school. I played sports and stayed as active as possible just to keep my mind off moving all the time. I also had to make sure I was perfect with everything. My hair had to be perfect. My clothes had to be perfect. It was a way to get attention, but my grades and my success started to decline.

Back in these days, Leominster and Fitchburg always collided. I knew Fitchburg people, and then I got close to Leominster people, so I got stuck in the middle. My first day at Leominster High I was in my second class of the day when I saw a guy popping his head in the classroom window. This guy ended up becoming my third high school boyfriend. I would continue this story, but for now, onto the next chapter.

CHAPTER 4

Miss Promiscuous

I got this amazing phone call. It was my best friend announcing to me she was getting married. She asked me to be one of her bridesmaids. Of course, being full of excitement, I said yes. When her wedding day came, our dresses were a beautiful pink, off shoulder. And it was a beautiful, hot summer day. All of us girls got together, and one of them happened to be a girl I went to high school with. We did not get along too well.

She approached me at the wedding and told me how beautiful I looked. She complimented on everything about me and how I looked. She asked me what I did for work. After I told her, she said, "Why don't you come work with me?"

I asked what she did, and she told me she was a dancer. I then laughed and said, "No way."

She then told me about all the money she would make, the drinking and some drugs, and that it's a fun job. I then asked her, "When can I try it out?"

She told me she would pick me up the following weekend and we would go together. She said I could just sit and watch at first to see how I would feel about it. I then had a captain and coke and started to feel good. After her dance set, she asked me what I thought. I then told her, "We drove all this way and I'm ready."

I went in the back where she gave me an outfit to wear since we were the same size. This strip club was a two-hour drive from where I lived, so I felt safe and free knowing I could dance without no one knowing me. I put on the outfit which made me look like a schoolgirl, along with black high-heeled boots that I had to practice walking in. I had no clue what I was doing, but I wanted the money and attention, knowing that no perverted man could touch me and that I had control over my own body.

I took a line of cocaine and a shot of alcohol. I walked over to the DJ and gave him the songs for my twenty-minute set. This club had two sides: one with full nudity and the other partial nudity. I danced in the full nudity part. I went up when I heard my first song playing and I just started to strut my stuff. I slowly took off my shirt, and when I did, I heard whistling and yelling, but all my eyes saw were the dollar bills. There were at least 100 to 150 men in this place.

When they were yelling, they were in crowds. I would go to different spots to collect the money, show off my breasts, and do other poses, which I am not proud of. I had the DJ play mostly rock music which I knew the guys liked. Now I start to strip everything off my body, not caring what anyone thought. I knew that I couldn't be touched in any way.

After my set was over, I walked down the stairs off the stage, and there was my bouncer waiting for me to escort me to the back room. Right there and then I said this was the place for me. I felt powerful, beautiful and thought I knew what I was getting myself into. As my night ended the owner approached me and asked if I was coming back. I laughed and he said, "We would like to have you here at least four or five nights a week."

I was told I had to pick a stage name, and I chose Adrianne because of Rocky so I could make it fun. I worked for them for two months, and as I was there, they liked me so much that I got my own dancing box in the front as people were entering. I was the first girl they would see. I then found out they had a room called the champagne room. I was approached by the owner who told me there were men who wanted me in the champagne room. I was very leery, but I did it anyway and made triple the money in less time. This kind of life was how I liked to live at this point.

One night I left early. The bouncers would walk us out to our cars and demand that we do not stop anywhere local and to just get on the highway to get home. That night there was a gas station in view from where I worked. I would not have made it home and had to get gas. It was a gas station that had a small window area to pay. The man working asked me if anyone was in the car with me.

I said, "No, why?"

He told me he thought he had seen someone's head moving. As I turned and looked at my car, my back door was flung open and there was a small butterfly jackknife on the ground. Then the gas attendant and I saw a man running into the woods. That was the end of the life I thought I would enjoy. I never went back.

I couldn't explain how scared I was. I could have been killed. It was an awakening that any girl or woman would never turn back to that life again.

I then began to feel dirty and stupid once I stopped and got back into reality: a real job. I did not want to make these little paychecks I called them. But then again it was money, and I am not going to get killed. I felt funny, but I can tell you it was hard to act normal. I was a dancer; I could not stop flirting and showing my body off in tight jeans and low-cut shirts. I lived to be seductive, to seduce men, to have them lust after me, and I could not get enough.

Why? Because I knew I had experienced being a player. I was played with as a child from a man. I wanted revenge, so I would sleep around and hurt innocent men and have no remorse. I had a lot of friends, and I would do these things secretly: the flirting, the dominant attitude I had was just so amazing to me. I was almost like on a drug—a love drug. if I caught a man's or a boy's attention, I knew I won!

I caught him. I could not stop. I wanted more attention, and I did not care who I hurt and why they hurt. If they had a girlfriend or a wife, it was not my business. Just giving him the pleasure of seeing my face or body, I knew that's all it took. I was almost numb. I loved (or thought I loved) who I was dating, but I never knew love. I always knew revenge and hurting the opposite sex. I was programmed to have no respect for myself or who I was dating. Now that I am older, I know now all of this I am sharing was not okay.

Please know many things have happened to me. I will continue to tell you some of the things you hear that may relate to you or appall you.

CHAPTER 5

Young Mom

I was only nineteen when I met my oldest daughter's father (at sixteen) and had a lot of fun. I moved to Leominster, and he was the boy popping his head in and out of my classroom window. The boy who fell head over heels for me. But you know what I did. At that time, we just really clicked. I then began my messy life: I moved out of my aunt's house and moved in with him and his family because he had his own basement bedroom. It was huge. I practically lived there all the time, so that's where I ended up.

We had a ton of friends. We both worked really hard but partied really hard as well. Every time we started our day, we could have been up all night and went to work the next day. We were young. All we wanted was fun and work. We would have house parties, keg parties, bar parties, and pool parties. It just never ended, and we both loved to be with all our friends and smoke weed and drink, on top of other things, which I will speak of later on in this book. I never had a boring day or night. We were inseparable: always looking out for each other. I then realized the partying was turning into more of an addiction than fun. It was almost as if we could not function without always being around drinking and other activities that were fun but not healthy.

I decided to join a gym with a friend of mine. She was looking tone, and we were doing the same exercises together. We were doing crunches like you would not begin to imagine. I noticed she was getting what we would call a six-pack. I was shocked because we were going the same days and doing the same exercises. I noticed my arms and legs were very defined, but my stomach was very bloated, almost like you were going to have a period.

I then missed my period, so I bought a pregnancy test and it was positive. You could just imagine what was going through my head. It was not what most would want to ever say, but I was almost in an abortion clinic. I could not do it! I then told the father I stopped partying while he still did; it did not bother me. I knew our ages, and it was completely normal for him to still want to continue. We had a lot of friends, so why take that away from someone else?

As the months went by, I worked with his mom. I made good money, and through my whole pregnancy, it was difficult because I had very bad morning sickness. But I pressed through being so young.

I had many friends who supported our decision to keep this beautiful cherub. We had an amazing baby shower. Both of our families came together and loved us and our decision. I was told I could take castor oil and that would induce my labor because I was impatient and knew I was going to have her soon. Yes, we had a baby girl. I had the worst experience with labor pain and being given Demerol, which was a very big needle that went very deep into your outer upper thigh; it was the worst pain ever more so than pushing.

Here we were two new parents but still young ourselves, not understanding that we couldn't party anymore or live our lives. We were very spoiled with friends babysitting, and his mother would always be there because we lived in the same house. We were with our daughter but still got to do the things kids our age still did. I sometimes looked back and wished that we were not so fortunate to always have babysitters. We were doing bad drugs and becoming addicted to a drug that was not so intense in the beginning of use; it just took a hold of you so unexpectedly. We did it socially, then it became very often; almost nightly it caused paranoia and wanting more and more when it was gone, even our hard-earned money.

A lot of times we would be with other people just sharing, and it was not a very social drug. We were caught in a snare that was so hard to escape from. We found ourselves continuing to buy and go to a certain guy's house. It was a very bad situation as we both had good jobs and a new baby. What were we thinking, going to the next party or out at night—it was sad.

I knew that this was becoming bad because I was always working and coming home, seeing my daughter's dad doing it alone in the bathroom. I would get so upset or I knew he would be at a certain person's house. I would head over there, and there he was with about half a house full of people who enjoyed the high as well.

The only way out was to leave. It was the hardest decision, but I could not take this addiction anymore. I started to feel ugly and especially a horrible mother. I then moved back in with my aunt who raised me, and it was not that easy. She had a son (my daughter's age), and it was difficult to be around her when everything bugged my aunt. I then started getting in touch with an old friend from Lunenburg and started another relationship. I knew this person for a long time, and we started to date. He had no kids, and I was always at his house with my daughter, who was around two, and that did not work either.

I was a mother, lost and sad, but just continued to chase friends, drugs, alcohol, and dating. I could not look at myself other than to get ready to go to work or get ready to go out for the night. I had no self-esteem, almost just living in a spinning wheel going around and around, not thinking about being a mom. I knew how selfish it was. I needed to find a babysitter to go to the next event so I wouldn't lose my relationships with friends or men.

If I could have done life over again, I would have. But I know sharing this will let you know you are not alone. Some of us were raised with love and morals, and some were raised like me, alone and afraid. *Mom* was not what I should have been called. It should have been *monster*. I did everything I could to change her diapers and make sure she was safe and fed, but I still had this fantasy in my head that I was missing so much more out in this world. Sadly, I was mistaken.

CHAPTER 6

Failed at Marriage

I now met my husband at a place I was working at. I met him through one of my uncles who worked at the same place we did. He actually got me the job. I was living with my aunt still, and I now had my daughter in a day care while I worked full-time, and it was a place where the guys flirted with the girls back and forth. Pretty much like high school.

I believe I was twenty-three when I worked here. I met my first husband, and I thought he was cute in his own way and had an incredible sense of humor. He just made me laugh all the time. Something I was not used to. I was always miserable and doing drugs still on the side or drinking. Just always looking to numb the break-ups and bad-mom syndrome. We started to date, and he did not do drugs and barely drank. And I was like, *This is what me and my daughter need. No bad things and just being a family*, or at least knowing he accepted myself and her. I then moved out with him and lived at his brother's right across from where we worked together.

One night we got out of work late, and as we were walking toward the condo, I saw a bunch of fire trucks and police cars. And I don't know if I have a gift or just a sense of being a mom, but I said to my boyfriend (at the time we were not married yet), "They are at our place!"

And he said, "No way!"

I said, "Oh my god. They are!"

My two-year-old only daughter was gone, and the bedroom she was sleeping in caught on fire. I screamed out to his brother and his wife, "Where is she!"

I was in such a panic! They said, "In the ambulance outside"; I was like, "No one is with her."

And that is when I knew how much being her mom was so important.

The rule was to never shut the door all the way, and that night they did. The alarm clock caught on fire, and so did the bed. And it was a miracle they said she moved down to the other end of the bed. I did not know God, but I just thanked him and didn't even realize I was speaking. God heard me. It was a miracle something or someone was already protecting her.

Now after that happened, we found our own place in a great neighborhood. We actually lived above another uncle of mine, and as we lived there and settled in, life was great. And then I found out I was pregnant. Everyone was excited, but again I had the worst morning sickness. I could not smell anything without wanting to puke. I was a cigarette smoker, and my uncle would go into the hallway to smoke, and my poor boyfriend would have to let him know the smell was making me throw up. My uncle was not too happy, but I'm sure he understood.

We then decided to get married. I believe I was three months along when we did. We had the big wedding, the white dress, limo, bridesmaids, etc. The fairy-tale wedding, the one you see everyone read about. It was more stressful than fun. It truly was. Pictures and not having enough time to say hello to people and talk for more than five minutes. And it just went by so fast.

You were pretty much paying to get married. It was not under God; it was more like, this is a party. I thought I was in love, but I was so young. And remember, I was never counseled or medicated for my abuse, so I'm just going with life. I didn't know any better. We had a great time. I believe we didn't have a honeymoon, so we just went back home exhausted but loved the fact we had a great celebration.

A few weeks after we were married, one of my aunts contacted me and said, "We are selling my Victorian house. You should look into buying it from us."

I was super excited because this house was beautiful. They helped us do the paperwork, and my aunt who raised me warned us and said, "Don't do it. They are asking too much. You're getting ripped off."

I, at that time, was on top of the world thinking I knew everything, and to my surprise, my aunt was right. We purchased the home that should have been way lower priced like I had been told. Therefore, our lesson was learned the hard way: we were ripped off from a family member whom I thought loved and cared about me but instead thought about themselves. The problems that occurred were very expensive. We didn't have enough money to fix all the things that they knew were needed and never had an inspector come before we purchased because we trusted.

We then began to just pay the mortgage like we were supposed to, but my husband at this time liked to spend money as well as me. So our payments began to stop because we knew we couldn't fix the house, which began to ruin our marriage.

Now living here for almost a year, we had our daughter. She was such an easy birth and couldn't have asked for a more peaceful baby. I worked days, and her father worked nights, so that part of our stress was relieved. We had many family members over the house and actually had the aunt (who told us not to purchase the home) move in on the first floor of our Victorian home. Now with her income coming in, it was just more money to spend. My husband at the time was a very nice man, but his spending habits and my spending habits did not work. We began to argue, and I was not happy.

One day he came home, and I told him that I wanted a divorce. I believe we were married for a year and a half of that. He was not happy, but he left, and we had a civil divorce. We had to sell the house, and we beat foreclosure. I now am a divorced single mother of two from two different men.

Did I fail? Did I make the wrong decisions? *No.* Here is why.

CHAPTER 7

I Know Everything

I was now twenty-four years old looking around, saying to myself, "Hey, I know everything. I am going to move onto this next chapter of my life."

That was probably going to be the wildest ride of this entire book.

I was still working in the same place as my ex-husband. I met a guy closer to my age whom I was very attracted to, and he was attracted to me as well. We then started to date. I was living in Leominster in a condo, and he was living with some roommates. I would say two months after dating, he moved in. I took a bartending job, and he took a plumbing job. I made awesome money as well as he. He liked to smoke pot, and then I started and liked it. We were functioning partiers just like my first daughter's dad.

I loved my bartending job. I found myself telling him to get the girls from day care so I could stay after work and drink. I would miss dinnertime, and everybody at the bar that I knew would keep buying me a drink, and this continued for about a few months. He then asked me, "Please stop or this isn't going to work."

I then stopped during the week, but my daughters' dads would take them on the weekends, and I would stay until whenever I wanted after work.

We both had a friend that we knew who dealt crack cocaine, and that was our new ride. We worked to buy it, and the devil made sure we never were broke. We lived with barely any sleep but had good days because we knew that we were going to be doing it at night. We began to isolate ourselves. We pretended at every family event, and we pretended in front of the girls that we were happy and life was great. But deep inside we were two addicts not knowing we were addicts.

I would always know (after the girls went to bed) it was our time to just smoke and get paranoid half the time, hoping they would not wake up, and they never did. I still could not believe waiting for the text or the callbacks, wanting more and more. It was the devil's realm just living to look forward to the next hit. It was the sickest I have ever lived.

This man and I broke up for a while. We were very active together, and it was getting bad. I still had my bartending job and met a regular there that was good friends with the owner, and we started to date. No smoking crack cocaine, now just snorting sometimes living the wildlife, not caring as long as I was happy putting all these chemicals in my body to numb the mess I had just left. We had fun. He took me on trips, and we would travel everywhere, just had a complete blast. But in the meantime, my girls were left with their dads, so I could just take off all the time. It truly was not okay.

Then this man opened a bar of his own and started to date others, and I was not having it, so I told him I was done. Also he told me he could not have any more children because he was fixed. I was very thankful for that, knowing I would not get pregnant, I thought.

I then stayed by myself and just stayed working there at the same bar regardless of whether he would come in or not. My ex contacted me and said he needed to come over. The guy who was dealing the drugs to us had been murdered, and I went to high school with him, and my ex was very close to him not just due to the drugs but in general. I am respecting the family. I will not explain to much detail on his death, but it was really bad!

I was in shock, and just to make this worse, the couple who murdered him came to our place to bring the drugs, and we asked why they were here and why our friend was not answering his phone. And they said he was sleeping. I couldn't believe we had these monsters over our home. God spared us and our lives. Now that I look back, I am thankful.

I was now back with my ex, and things were going well, and after a few months, I found out I was pregnant. We were shocked but very happy hoping this was going to stop the madness. He still continued to smoke. I couldn't, but not as much as we used to. I worked up until my due date. I loved this baby girl. I loved all my girls. This little one was my biggest: she was almost eight pounds. That was big for me. I was only five-foot-three and a tiny girl.

He came from a big family as well as I did. This little one got so much attention and love. So did my other girls from his family very happy, and things were seeming normal—until she grew a little and then we preceded to continue right back into the trap of the drugs again. It was crazy, always coming home with it after he came home from work and sometimes he would do some before he would get home.

We would then begin to argue if it was almost gone. It was so sad that was all that mattered to us! Remember, I did not know who God was. I would not care about anything else but the time to get that hit, and sometimes we would go in the bathroom back and forth just to do it and to not make it obvious to the kids.

We started to fight so much the drug was starting to kill us inside and out. I was getting severe panic attacks, and things were happening to me mentally I could not function. While home alone during the day, I actually was at a point where I tried to kill myself. I was prescribed Zoloft, but I took the whole bottle. He grabbed my daughter and left, not before saying, "Have fun dying."

We were at a point we just hated each other. The only thing that had kept us connected was the drug. It was not a social drug, so when you had someone to do it with you, you felt less of a loser.

Going back to the Zoloft, I laid on the couch, and I just began to see blackness: A reaper form in a cloak with a black cat looked like it was coming out of the wall. I was dying, and I was not heading to see Jesus. I was on my way to hell.

I panicked and called 911; they came and took me and said, "If you don't drink this black charcoal drink, we are going to have to put a tube down your throat and pump your stomach."

I freaked out and drank. Thank God. It was gross, but the medicine came out of my system not in a pleasant way but enough to save my life.

I was not put in a program or considered unfit as a mother because thankfully no one was home, so my kids had no idea what happened. They thought I had the flu, so again God was there, and I did not even realize he had been with me through all of these unspeakable actions.

A few weeks after I started having really bad anxiety, my little one-year-old had a fever and she had a seizure, so I had to call 911. When I did, I started to panic, and they had to give me a paper bag to breathe in. I believe I was going back to when my oldest was in a fire. She was looking at me the same way my oldest was just blank, almost in a trance. I was so scared, but she made it through. I then said out loud after my suicide attempt, "This relationship is over."

CHAPTER 8

Trying It on My Own

I then kicked him out and knew I could not afford where I was living. I had my real mom move in, which was not a good idea. She was still active on drinking, but she was telling me otherwise, saying she had been sober, which I thought she was. She started to tell me to go out and take some time for myself, and then I would say I had plenty of time to myself. She would stay with my daughters while I would just go out with my friends to just feel normal and go to parties. I was, I believe, twenty-eight at the time. I knew it was wrong but continued walking and running with the wrong crowd that I thought would pull me out of so many messed-up things going on in my mind. I was completely selfish, leaving my kids, thinking I was going to meet the man of my dreams and stop doing drugs. But that was definitely not the case.

As winter approached, I was not able to pay rent, and things were starting to spiral out of control. I had put all of my and daughters' belongings in the basement for storage, and I believe we hit a below-zero temperature. Someone came to take a look at the building I was living in, and when they went into the basement, they moved a piece of wood from the window which let cold air in, and it froze the pipes.

The next day I heard what sounded like a river, and it was a pipe that exploded, so I called my ex (who I kicked out). He was a plumber. He said, "Sorry, you're on your own."

Everything was covered. The water was coming up the stairs almost into my house. I had to call the fire department and water department to shut the water down. I cried. Everything was gone: memories and all things that my two daughters had that meant a lot to them, including baby pictures and all these important documents and things that were passed to me from my now-passed-away grandmother.

I could not explain to you how much it really affected me and my girls. It was just like a fire. Nothing could have been recovered. We had no running water. I was getting evicted, so my landlord would not fix it. So I was buying gallons of water a day to cook and flush the toilet. We had friends where I could take us to shower and bathe, but by board of health with daughters who were small, I had an emergency. I had to leave. I put my name on an emergency housing list. They gave me a hard time. Then my grandfather stepped in, and we finally found a place, and my rent was low to my income.

I then had to let them know if I was going to make more money, and when I did, they raised the rent. I could not believe where honest gets you; I was mortified. I tried to fight that, but there was no win until I received a phone call. It was a girl whom I called my sister. I never believed in God at this time, but why on earth did everything go the way it did? Why was I spared? I was sent to people all the time, and I could not believe how on time it happened.

CHAPTER 9

A Chance?

I heard on the other line, "Hi, Crystal."

It was my sister. She asked me if I wanted to be roommates with her. She had two extra bedrooms, my two girls had bunk beds, and I had my own room. For a hundred dollars cheaper and I was also closer to work so I did not have to travel far, and friends and family were also closer. I had worked two jobs, would work in the morning and then leave there and have maybe an hour to get dressed for my second job. It was nonstop, but I had to make the money. I was all I had.

I also received child support, which was very helpful, and on my weekends, I could work doubles because the girls would go with their dads. I was never really exhausted because I was younger and knew bills were due and I had no other options. I actually went on a few dates while I lived there, but nothing serious. I was focused on me and the girls. I believe I was single for a year. I really enjoyed the independence, but I was also missing the companionship, so I just continued working until someone I would be interested in came along.

I saw this girl whom I had not seen in years, and she said, "Come to my house." By coincidence, she only lived two streets over. "I am having a Halloween party, and before we go, we are all getting ready here."

I said, "It's last minute. I don't have a costume."

She said a friend of hers would lend me one. So I saw this guy who made sure I could not see him pass by me while the girls were doing my makeup. I said, "Who was that? He went by so fast."

She said, "That's just my cousin."

I just laughed and yelled out, "Okay."

We then all piled up in the cars and headed to the hall, and I noticed a guy dressed all up in camouflage, and he was buying everyone from the house a drink at the bar. I approached him because I was far from shy and said, "Hey. I was there too. Where is my drink?"

He then laughed and said, "Go ahead and get one. It's on me."

I laughed and walked away and continued to have fun with the girls, not thinking this guy was going to approach me back. This was my friend's cousin, the one that went by me very fast at the house, so to all of us, it was very funny. The party was ending, and that was how he and I met. We all went to another late-night bar, dancing and getting a little frisky and not having a care in the world.

I then gave him my number, and he knew I was roommates with my sister, so we started to hang out. He had his own place, him and his dog, but it was only a one-bedroom. I knew when my girls were gone, I was continuing to go to his house because at the time, my sister had her friends over a lot on weekends to party and hang out. We started to argue because she was allowing people to sleep in my bed while I was not home and, I believe, in the girls' beds as well. So all hell broke loose.

I believe after a week or two later she moved, and he moved in with me and started to help with the girls and paying rent. My car was falling apart, and he actually had an extra one in the garage that was just about brand-new, so I had that and was so much happier knowing it was not going to break down. I knew my car was on its way out.

The car actually died a few days after. He offered for me to use the car, and I was very hesitant, because I did not want to look desperate with two daughters and needing things. Remember, I have been independent for a year. He had a very good job and encouraged me to do one job, and again, I said, "No, I could use the money."

He said, "You get child support, there is your other income."

I thought about it and agreed.

I was now able to spend more time with the girls and focus on them and family. He came from a very big family with the same parents who got married when he and his one sister were only young. I was thinking, *Okay, this guy comes from a good background.* He never had drug addiction or alcohol issues, so I was relieved and felt okay, I have been sent to someone who was "normal."

When I say *sent*, it was not because I believed in God at that time. There I was spared again, thinking and believing it was going to be this amazing new future for the girls and me. I did have three daughters at this time, but my oldest was living with her dad. That was why you heard me saying two. But those who were living with me, he took care of as his own, with no kids of his own. I really believed this was the one in my life. He took on every burden I had financially and stability, and I knew he loved me with all his heart. He told me all the time. I did notice he has a temper, not just a little anger but a lot of moods. He did have a lot of head injuries from sports, so I knew they were due to concussions.

One night I was just sitting in the living room, and this woman was speaking about her life, and the first thing she said was, her father molested her, and I knew for some reason I was supposed to listen. I noticed there was scripture on the screen. I would ignore it, thinking I don't need this. I need to hear what she was saying about her life. It was all about me, almost like this was not happening. This was not real.

I then started making sure I would watch her almost every day. Her name is Joyce Meyer. She was helping me and the guy I was with at the time. She would just let me watch her, and I did not make a big deal about it. I did not believe in God. So I just looked at her like a counselor of some sort. We were together for a year and found out I was pregnant. It happened so fast we were still living in the same apartment. We were shocked but at the same time happy. It was hard to explain.

Our families were shocked but anxious and happy as well. I had the worst ending of a pregnancy. I was bedridden, only able to drink water. I would drink a twenty-four pack of water in about four days. Never in my life would I have ever thought I would drink that much. It was unreal. I was craving it. I was afraid I would drown her. Yes, another girl! Four girls, but they were all beautiful. I could not explain to you how hectic it was, but at the same time I was loving it.

We started to realize we were growing and needed a bigger place. He had a lot of relatives that had a lot of connections. We actually bought the house his cousin owned where we first met (with me getting ready for that Halloween party). We were so excited. The kids were too. He was a carpenter, so he remodeled everything, and it was beautiful. A little hectic on timing, but we made it.

The man I was with was always making good money and always waiting to make another dollar. He was and still is a hard worker. He was an amazing provider but always tired. He wanted me to stay home with our daughters. He called my girls his own as well. But his work was making him more and more stressed. The bills would pile up, and he would explode. We would argue all the time, and sometimes the screaming was so bad I started to get panic attacks. It was becoming overwhelming for me. I knew we would get through all of this, but when he got angry, you did not know if he would throw something or hurt me. It was very scary.

I knew we had a daughter, and I was not going to let her not have her dad in her life like my other daughters. I was starting to feel like a loser and blamed myself for his stress and anger. I would always scream back to defend myself. It became hell, a literal hell for all. Our home was so big I let my biological mother, who was sober, move in. She paid rent and was sick with one of those twenty-four-hour running oxygen machines but still addicted to scratch tickets, always buying them with her state money, always asking me to go to the store to buy them, and when she won, it was, "Can you go get me more?" It was cyclical.

I was beginning to get stressed out. So he would come home from work, and there I was, miserable because of the drama, and I never really knew. We never lived simple lives. We always helped people and put our relationship last.

Then she left, and here came an addict cousin I had living with us. She had nowhere to go again. We welcomed more problems into our lives and thought again we were helping. I was lied to all the time babysitting an adult addict. It was so horrible it caused my girls to want to not be around as well as the father of my daughter.

CHAPTER 10

Trying to Make It

I had my older daughter want to move back in. I believe she was seventeen. She also had a boyfriend who was having home issues. So of course we kicked out my addict cousin, and here comes my daughter's boyfriend. We really loved him. He was a good kid. He spent Christmas with us; my daughter seemed to be happy. I guess she wasn't, and we had to accept their breakup. I still saw him around all the time now. I understand now why they broke up.

Lesson learned: as a mother or father, do not get attached to your daughters' boyfriends. But then again I could say the same for my relationships had not lasted that long or were unhealthy.

After all was done and it was just us as a family in the house, I decided to take college classes online. I did awesome. I started taking business classes, and I would get paid for them because I had kids, so it was very beneficial. I was enjoying them and made time, and one night, out of the blue, the guy I was with received a phone call, saying his mother was in the hospital. He left, and he called me and told me she passed. I was very close to her. I died inside myself.

That really changed things. Everything was happening so fast it was almost a dream. I thought he was joking because he always had a sense of humor. I know that sounds sick, but it was hard to believe. We had just seen her the day before at our house, folding clothes and laughing. She made it for her only granddaughter's first birthday. She passed the day after.

I'll always remember how much she loved me and my daughters. It was a feeling I never felt before. She baked with me, and we went everywhere together. I never wanted to do anything, and she made sure that I didn't just get lazy and move. She inspired me to take those college classes.

Unfortunately, I quit. I couldn't continue my education. I was helping her son get over his mourning and keeping the girls as occupied and happy as I could. It was sad my daughter did not get a chance to meet such an amazing woman. I then started to see us become less of a family because we missed her so much and did not know what to do. I believe we started to get behind on our mortgage due to him not working, so there was much turmoil.

CHAPTER 11

New Home

The man I was still living with (who lost his mom) let us know we were going to have to move into a one-bedroom right next door to us.

"What!"

Yes, he said that is what we all have to do until I build this house. This guy and I were going to split the sale, and we are all going to move in until it was sold. In the meantime, there were five of us in a one-bedroom with two dogs. We made it, but it was not easy and had to keep up every day due to the lack of space and walking room.

He was there every day and night for sixteen hours and sometimes twenty-four hours sleeping in there to continue to work so we could move in. I was thankful, but at the same time he was getting sick from not eating and sleeping properly, almost like a stick figure. We, as a family, were very worried. He then went and was checked out by a doctor and he was told he had a thyroid issue. They gave him medicine that he would not take as prescribed, and then he became sicker, which turned into "Graves' disease."

Watching someone try so hard and almost die was very hard, but the good news was that he was doing better at this point and taking it easy. As me and the girls were home, he came in and said, "Get ready to pack up. We are moving this weekend. It is now ready to go."

We were all excited and thankful. This was a remodeled two-family house. It came out beautiful, and it was just exciting to have space and bedrooms again.

We were now in and I was starting to, all of a sudden, ghost hunt. I did not know why I was just so interested. I guess, not knowing who God was, your mind just wandered and whatever you saw online, you wanted to try.

CHAPTER 12

Meeting the Devil

I found a local ghost-hunting group in my area and read their website. I was really intrigued. I really thought this was going to be good for me. A hobby, meeting new people, doing the right thing, etc. I did my first ghost hunt, and I noticed one of the girls would tell a spirit to go home or find the light or even offer a prayer.

Some of the guys in the group had a rock-cover band, and I was also going to those events as well. I was not a very good mother. I was always hoping to be. I just wanted to do things, to keep away. I did not want to stay away from my children. I was just in a horrible relationship.

The ghost-hunting group called me and let me know that we had a really big paranormal activity at a residence in another town. It was about fifteen minutes away. I let my family know and went. I had never experienced or seen so much evil in all my life. I saw orbs and things moved as well as a girl in our group who got choked.

Whatever was in this building was the devil himself. I could not tell you how scared I was to see a face come out of an orb. The families in this building were being tortured day and night. I did not realize that these spirits could attach themselves to people, and I was the victim.

I went home that night, and I believe a few days later I came down with the worst flu ever, one I could not wish on my worst enemy. My spine hurt to the touch. It was as if I was being stabbed over and over again. Symptoms that were not normal.

Our home started to fall apart. The fighting was so bad chairs were flying from being thrown at me, screaming, telling my children I was this awful person and I put things and people before them and they meant nothing to me.

I had to really walk on pins and needles. My whole family was against me for a long time. I then gave in and went to a couple therapy, and I let this therapist know what I was doing for a hobby.

"Ghost hunting."

He looked at me and said, "Why are you doing this?"

I said, "I wanted to help these souls go to heaven."

He then asked me, "How are you doing that?"

I said, "I don't know. Asking God to come and save them and take them there."

He looked me square in the eyes and said, "Do you know Jesus?"

I said, "No."

He said, "You cannot serve the devil and God. You need to choose."

The End

ABOUT THE AUTHOR

Crystal Holroyd is a wife, a mother of four beautiful daughters, and a grandmother. She loves to minister to other women and let them know how much Jesus loves them. She has a passion to help others with her testimony. She is a singer as well as a writer. She enjoys spending time with her family and their two dogs. She has an amazing relationship with Jesus, and she knows this book is what he has written through her.

This is her story, and without God helping her write this book, she would have never been able to finish. She resides in Massachusetts where she was born and raised.

CPSIA information can be obtained
at www.ICGtesting.com
Printed in the USA
LVHW030433220322
714056LV00009B/481

9 781685 171438